CELTIC AND OLD NORSE DESIGNS

COURTNEY DAVIS

DOVER PUBLICATIONS, INC.
Mineola, New York

Bibliographical Note

Celtic and Old Norse Designs is a new work, first published by Dover Publications, Inc., in 2000.

DOVER *Pictorial Archive* SERIES

This book belongs to the Dover Pictorial Archive Series. You may use the designs and illustrations for graphics and crafts applications, free and without special permission, provided that you include no more than ten in the same publication or project. For permission for additional use, please email the Permissions Department at rights@doverpublications.com or write to Dover Publications, Inc., 31 East 2nd Street, Mineola, New York 11501.

However, resale, licensing, republication, reproduction or distribution of any illustration by any other graphic service, whether it be in a book or in any other design resource, is strictly prohibited.

Library of Congress Cataloging-in-Publication Data

Davis, Courtney, 1946–
   Celtic and Old Norse designs / Courtney Davis.
       p. cm. — (Dover pictorial archive series)
   ISBN-13: 978-0-486-41229-0
   ISBN-10: 0-486-41229-6
       1. Decoration and ornament, Celtic—Themes, motives. I. Title. II. Series.

NK1264.D374 2000
745.4'089'916—dc21

00-031614

Manufactured in the United States by LSC Communications
41229613   2018
www.doverpublications.com

PUBLISHER'S NOTE

In this marvelous collection, drawn from numerous Celtic and Old Norse sources in the British Isles and Scandinavia, a rich selection of traditional Christian and secular designs is brought together. Some of the meticulously rendered designs were found in illuminated manuscripts, missals, and psalters of the Celtic Church (including the incomparable Book of Kells and the earlier Book of Durrow) and on Celtic stone crosses. Others are from runic inscriptions on stones, Norse sword hilts and personal ornaments, and the decoration of everyday artifacts such as bedposts, horse collars, and weather vanes. The sources of the designs are in Ireland; Scotland; Wales; Cornwall, Cumbria, Gloucestershire, Northumberland, Sutton Hoo (in Suffolk), and the Isle of Man in England; Denmark; Norway; and Sweden.

Created in the period from the 6th century to the 12th century A.D. (some of them during the 9th and 10th centuries, at the height of the Norse invasions and occupations of large areas of England and Ireland), the designs represent the six major periods of Old Norse decoration: the Broa/Oseberg, Borre, Jellinge, Mammen, Ringerike, and Urnes styles, as well as many generations of Celtic Christian ornament, chiefly elaborated in Ireland and Scotland.

(a) from bronze mirror; (b) from bronze mirror; (c) from bronze bowl; (d) and (e) from handles on spoons

(a) pattern from sword hilt; (b) Celtic stone cross; (c) Celtic stone cross; (d) from a gold torc (neck collar or chain)

(a) pattern from bronze mirror; (b) spiral design on sword hilt

Celtic spirals from various stone crosses

designs from various stone crosses of Ireland, Scotland, and Cornwall

a

b

c

(a) from the Celtic cross at Monasterboice, Ireland; (b) adapted from a cross in Cornwall;
(c) from cross at Monasterboice, Ireland

(a) from the Celtic cross at Golden Grove, Wales; (b) adapted from a cross shaft at Llantwit Major, Wales

(a) and (b) from a Scottish cross; (c), (d), and (e) from the Book of Kells; (f) from a Cornish stone cross

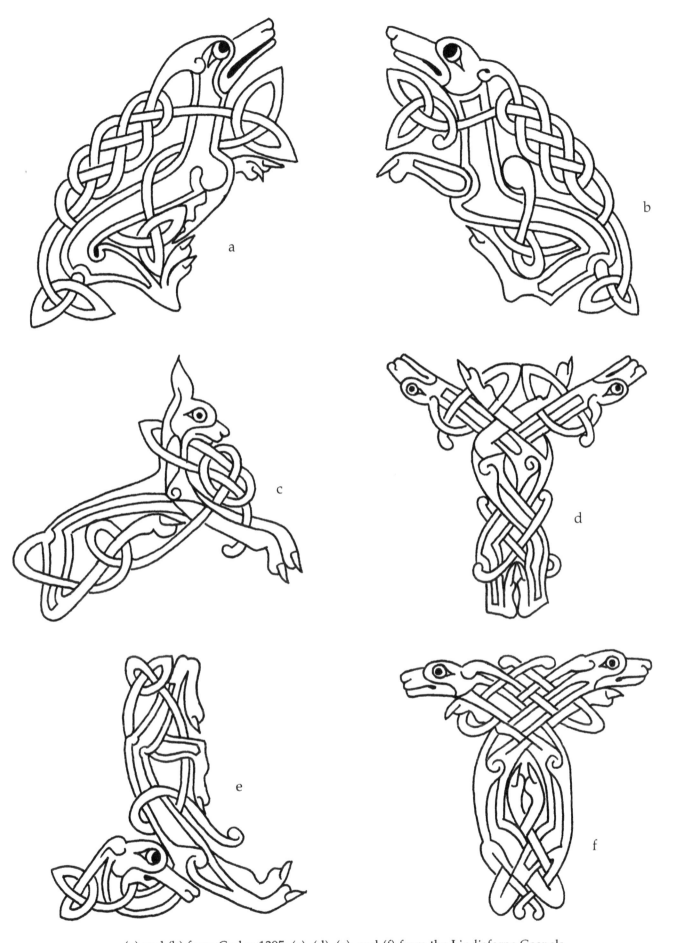

(a) and (b) from Codex 1395; (c), (d), (e), and (f) from the Lindisfarne Gospels

(a), (b), and (c) from the Book of Kells

from the Book of Kells

adapted from the Book of Kells

from the Coupar-Angus Psalter, Scotland

(a) initial from Winchcombe Psalter; (b) from St. Machan's Shrine; (c) and (d) from Cross of Cong; (e) from St. Machan's Shrine

(a) from Shrine of St. Lachtin's Arm; (b) and (c) from St. Machan's Shrine

(a) engraved axe from Jutland; (b) detail from St. Machan's Shrine

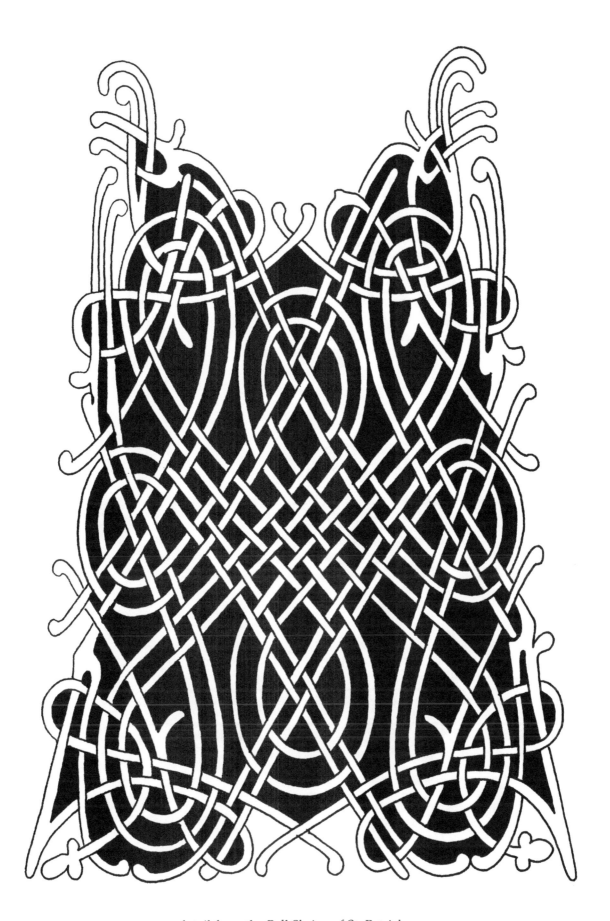

detail from the Bell Shrine of St. Patrick

(a) detail from the Cross of Lismore; (b) and (c) from the Bell Shrine of St. Patrick; (d) and (e) from St. Machan's Shrine

(a), (b), and (c) from the Bell Shrine of St. Patrick; (d) from the Cross of Cong

(a) from the Shrine of St. Lachtin's Arm; (b) initials from the Corpus Missell, Ireland

(a) from the Book of Durrow, Ireland; (b) design carved into antler, Ireland; (c) and (d) from the Sutton Hoo ship burial

(a) initial from the Chronicle of Marianus Scotus, Ireland; (b) and (c) from the Liber Hymnorum, Ireland

runic stone, Sweden

(a) Viking-style pendant; (b) two entwined beasts carved in stone

(a) Urnes-style bone pin; (b) figure of a bird on a whalebone line winder; (c) carved stone cist in Urnes style

(a) from the carved side of the Oseberg cart; (b) detail from a bedpost; (c) from an open-work brooch

ornament on a bronze-gilt weather vane

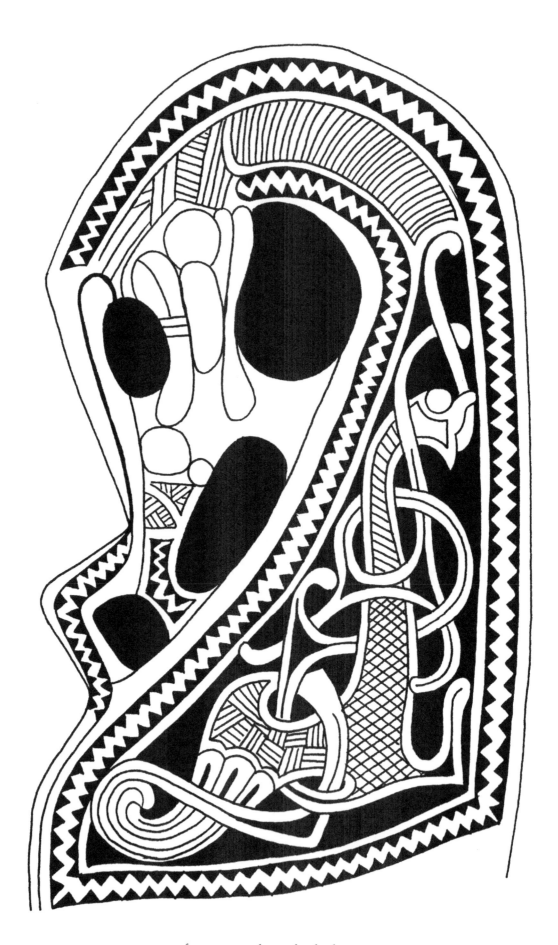

from a carved wooden bedpost

(a) and (c) Jellinge-style animals carved in stone, from the Isle of Man; (b) detail from a Mammen-style horse collar

(a) Borre-style strap end; (b) detail from Gosforth stone cross

entwined Urnes-style carved beasts

(a) brooch in English Urnes style; (b) Ringerike beast; (c) design from a fluted silver bowl from Gotland

(a) carved bone in the Mammen style of art; (b) detail from a horse collar

(a) and (b) adapted from a silver bowl in Gotland

34   *Old Norse Designs*

from the ornament on a sledge pole

(a) silver disk in the Jellinge style; (b) detail from a sledge pole in Oseberg

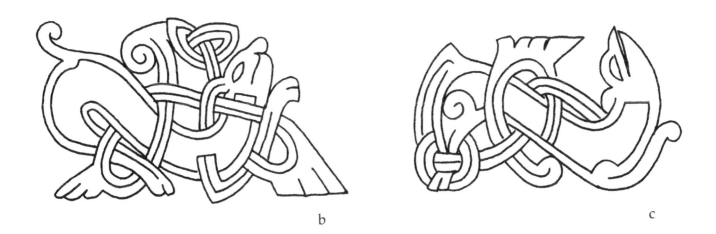

(a) "Great Beast" carved on a grave; (b) and (c) Jellinge-style animals carved in stone, from the Isle of Man

(a) silver crucifix; (b) and (c) details from mounts in the Broa style

animal heads carved on a whalebone plaque

a

b

(a) detail from a carved stone in Norway; (b) detail from a sledge pole in Oseberg

a

b

c

(a) detail from a horse collar; (b) two entwined beasts carved on a rune stone in Gotland;
(c) Jellinge-style animals carved in stone, from the Isle of Man

(a) detail from a brooch; (b) Gosforth Cross; (c) border detail from manuscript Junius II; (d) based on various brooch designs

Swedish rune stone

Detail from mount in the Broa style